Eclipse Begins!

Partial Phases

During the partial phase of the eclipse, part of the sun is still visible. Partial phases can only be viewed though certified eclipse glasses.

TOTALITY!

TOTALITY!

During totality, the moon completely covers the sun. It is incredible! If you are not in the path of totality, you will not see a total eclipse, but it will still be fun!

FUN FACT

If you are lucky enough to see "TOTALITY", you might see stars in the sky.

These "FUN FACT" boxes contain fun facts to share with your student.

Eclipse Ends

Use these diagrams and simple facts to explain
the eclipse to your TODDLER or PRESCHOOLER.

1. The MOON goes around the EARTH
2. The EARTH goes around the SUN

3. The SUN is big and very far away
4. The MOON is small and much closer to EARTH

FUN FACT

The Sun is about 93 MILLION MILES away from Earth.
The Moon is about 230 Thousand Miles away. To put
that in perspective... if the Sun was 100 yards away, the
Moon would only be 9 inches from the Earth

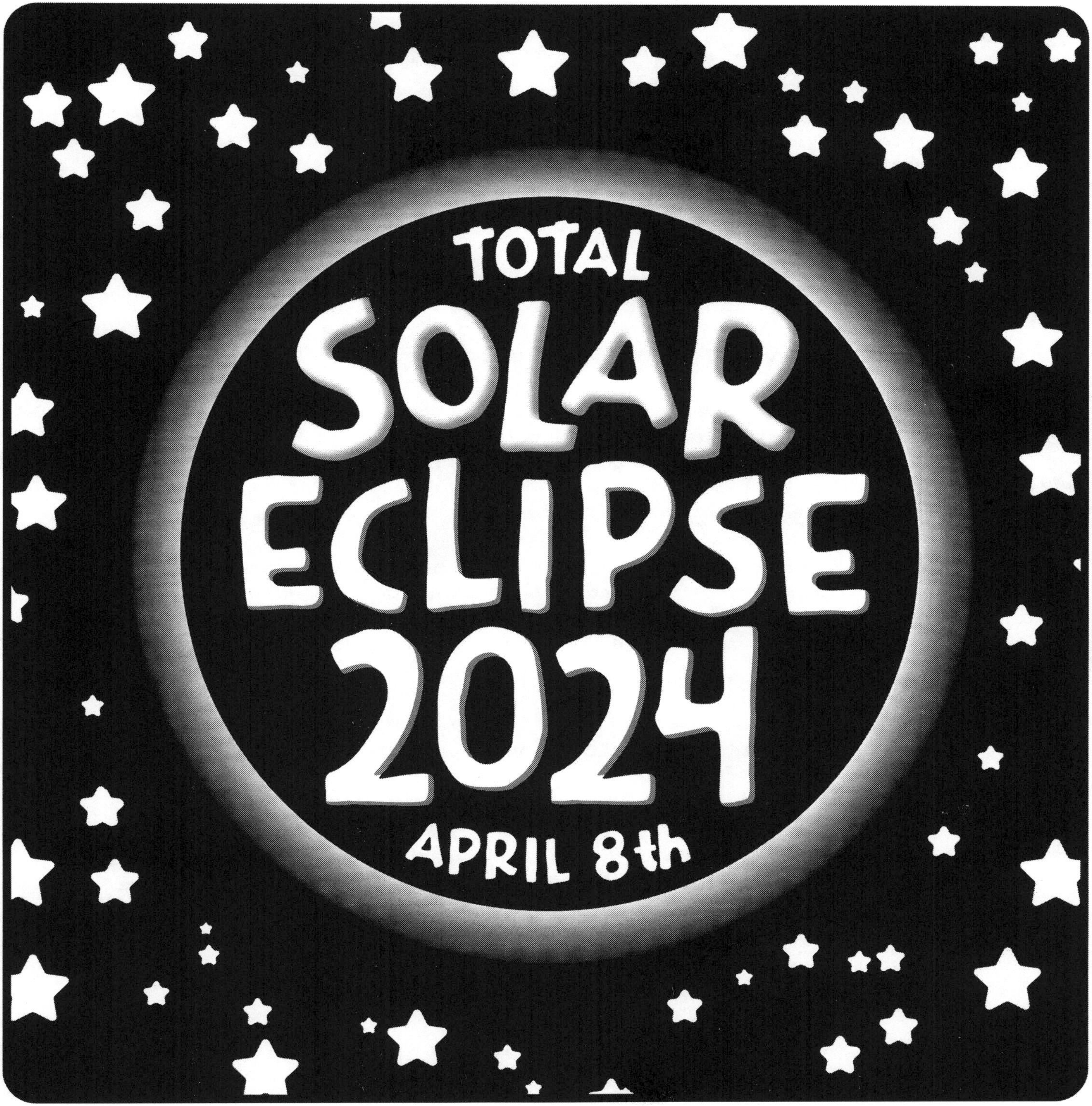
TOTAL
SOLAR
ECLIPSE
2024
APRIL 8th

A NOTE FOR PARENTS:

Hello! I am so glad you are interested in the April 8th, 2024 Solar Eclipse! And thank you for your interest in this book. I hope the weather cooperates and we can all witness the incredible eclipse!

About this book:

This GUIDED activity book is intended to be worked through WITH a toddler or preschooler that is learning to color or use a pencil. It is NOT intended for toddlers or preschoolers to complete on their own. Use it for quality time with your little student! As always, any page can just be scribbled on. if that is right for YOUR toddler.

Viewing a Solar Eclipse involves waiting. The partial phases of an eclipse are, honestly, not that exciting, especially for a 2-4 year old. This activity book can be used during the partial phases of the eclipse, to give you and your toddler something educational to work on together to pass the time. And when the eclipse is over, you will have this workbook to remember the shared experience.

This activity book contains a variety of early preschool level activities, such as counting to 10, tracing letters, pencil control skills, and color by number. As with anything designed for toddlers, some activities may be too easy, and some may be too hard. I hope you and your toddler find the activities of some value as a supplement to your other teaching.

I have purposefully kept the number of pages fairly minimal. My toddlers had a feeling of success when they "finished the whole book", and I hope that yours can too.

The most important thing is the ECLIPSE itself and the time you share with your child :)

One last thing... if clouds block the eclipse, it can be very disappointing. Have something else planned (that YOU can control) to look forward to if clouds spoil the day.

Fingers crossed for a clear day!

- Joshua Kemp (a.k.a. science teacher and homeschooling dad of 3)

5. From EARTH, the SUN and MOON look the same size

6. A SOLAR ECLIPSE happens when the MOON passes in front of the SUN

After you have explained the basics of a solar eclipse, ask your TODDLER or PRESCHOOLER if they can explain it to you, or to one of their stuffed animals :)

* This is a great strategy if you have never tried it. Toddlers sometimes enjoy explaining things to their stuffies – especially when you're not listening :)

FUN FACT The Sun is about 400 times farther away than the Moon, but its diameter is about 400 times larger than the Moon's. So from Earth, they look the same size in the sky! Isn't that awesome?!

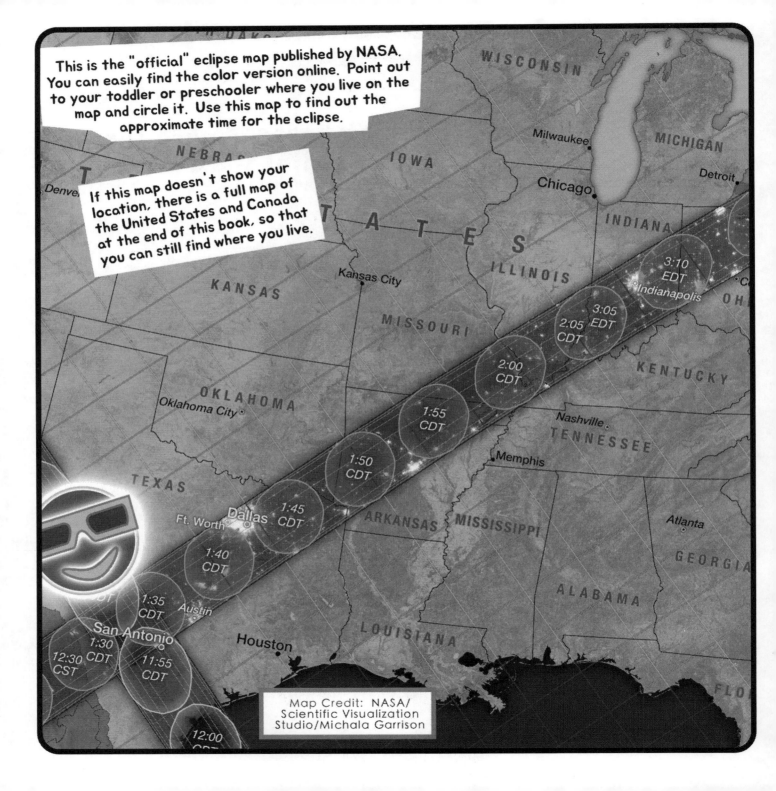

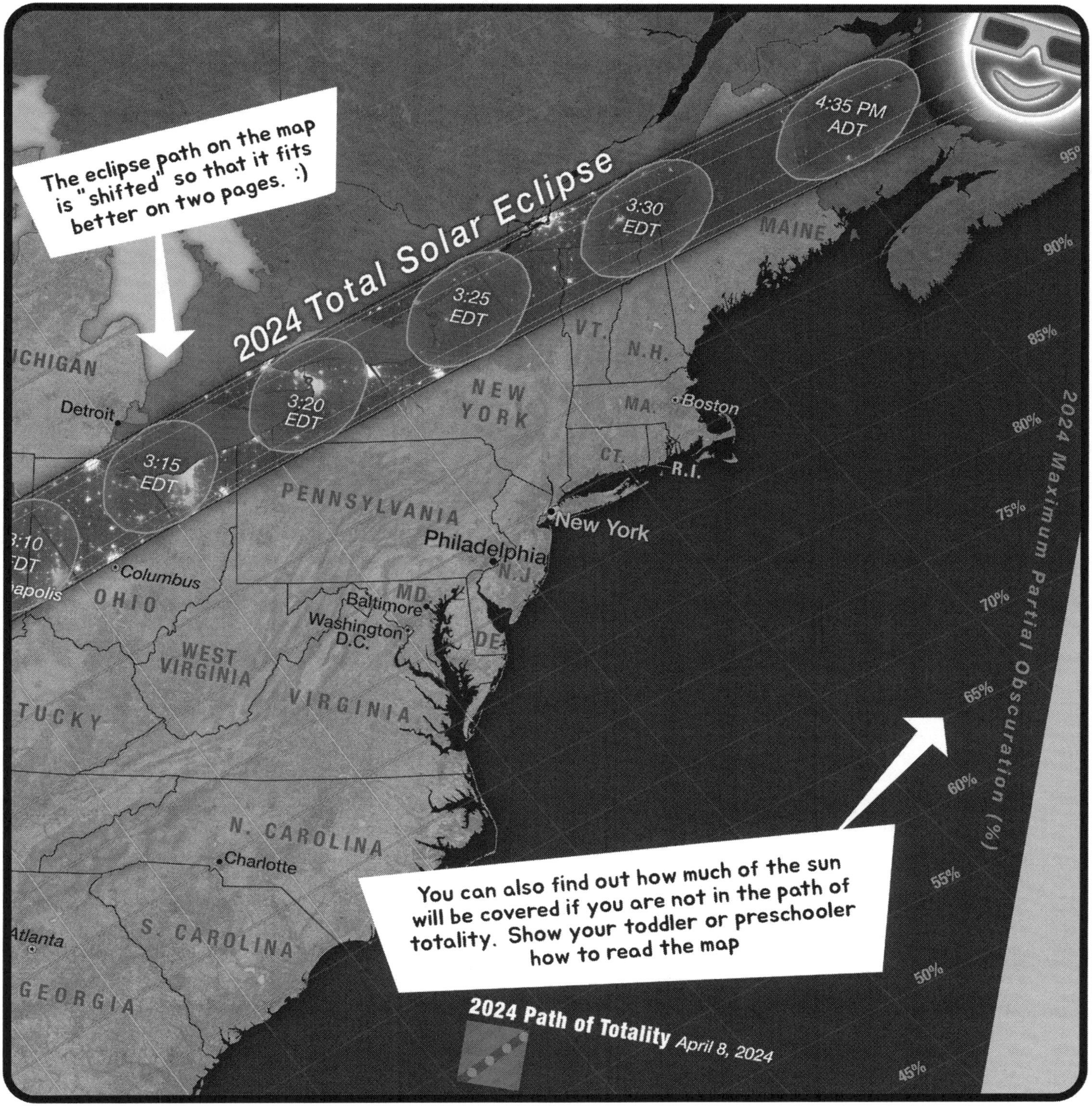

The eclipse path on the map is "shifted" so that it fits better on two pages. :)
2024 Total Solar Eclipse
4:35 PM ADT
3:30 EDT
3:25 EDT
3:20 EDT
3:15 EDT
3:10 EDT
MAINE
VT.
N.H.
NEW YORK
MA.
Boston
CT.
R.I.
New York
PENNSYLVANIA
Philadelphia
N.J.
MD.
Baltimore
Washington D.C.
DE.
Detroit
Columbus
OHIO
WEST VIRGINIA
VIRGINIA
N. CAROLINA
Charlotte
S. CAROLINA
Atlanta
GEORGIA
95%
90%
85%
80%
75%
70%
65%
60%
55%
50%
45%
2024 Maximum Partial Obscuration (%)
You can also find out how much of the sun will be covered if you are not in the path of totality. Show your toddler or preschooler how to read the map
2024 Path of Totality April 8, 2024

CONNECT THE LETTERS!

(Letter Recognition and Pencil Control)

DIRECTIONS: Connect the letters to spell:

SOLAR ECLIPSE APRIL 8 2004

GOOD LUCK!
Start Here

Many people will have solar eclipse glasses for this eclipse, and it is fun to "Design-Your-Own"!
Design and color some of the eclipse glasses WITH your toddler or preschooler. They love that!

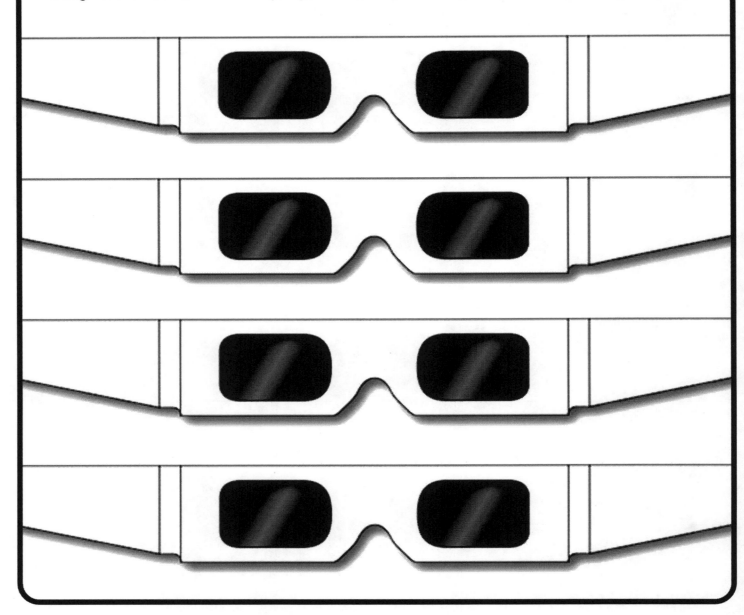

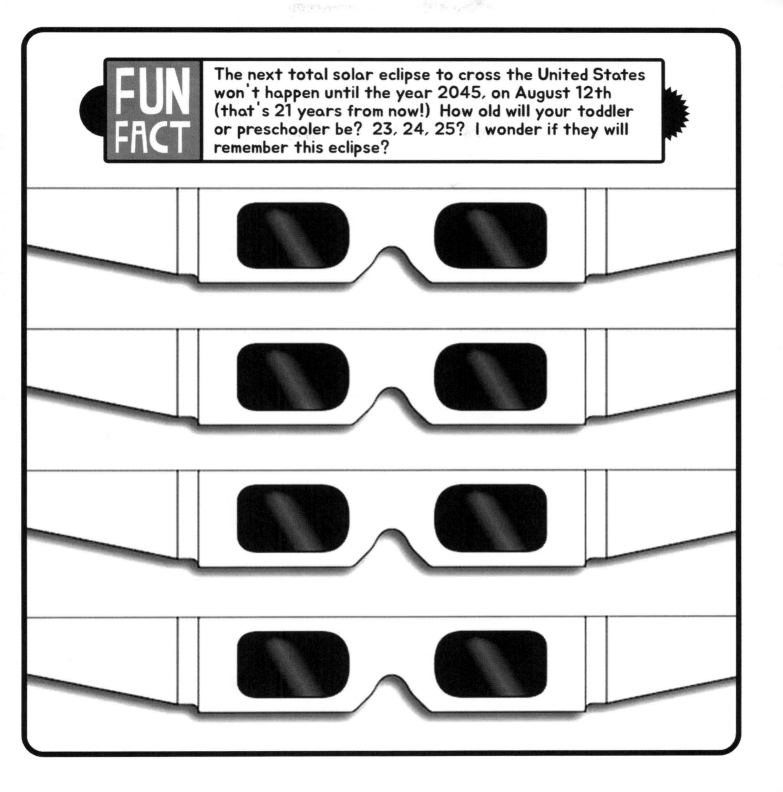

FUN FACT The next total solar eclipse to cross the United States won't happen until the year 2045, on August 12th (that's 21 years from now!) How old will your toddler or preschooler be? 23, 24, 25? I wonder if they will remember this eclipse?

Let's Play! : CONNECT THE DOTS Rocket Ship!
(Numbers and Pencil Control)

You are on a rocket ship traveling to 10 planets!
Can you travel to all 10 planets and make it back home again?
Start at the number 1 and try to follow the path all the way around the star.
Say each number as you go!

GOOD LUCK!!!

1

10

2

9

3

8

4

6

7

5

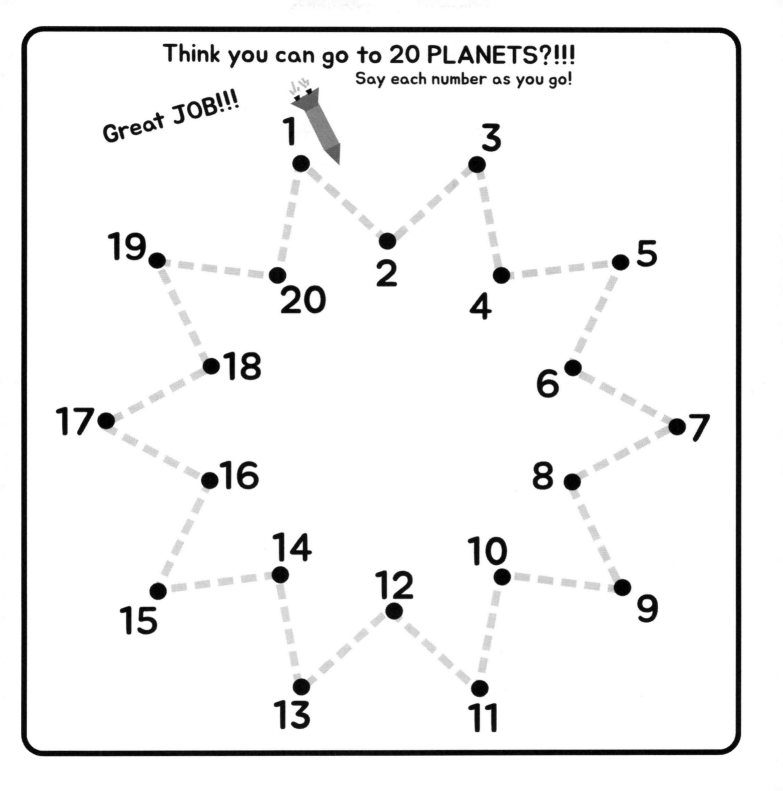

Let's Play...

I SPY COUNTING!!!

(Counting, Pencil Control, and Colors!)

directions: the correct number of objects from the list!

I spy some Suns! Can you circle 1 Sun with YELLOW?

I spy some planet Earths. Can you circle 2 Earths with GREEN?

I spy some Moons. Can you circle 3 Moons with BLACK?

I spy some solar eclipse glasses.
Can you circle 4 solar eclipse glasses with RED?

I spy many exclamation marks!
Can you circle 5 exclamation marks with BLUE?

FUN FACT Light from the Sun takes about 8 minutes to reach Earth. Light from the moon takes only about 1.3 seconds! to reach Earth. This gives you an idea just how much farther away the Sun really is than the Moon. WOW!

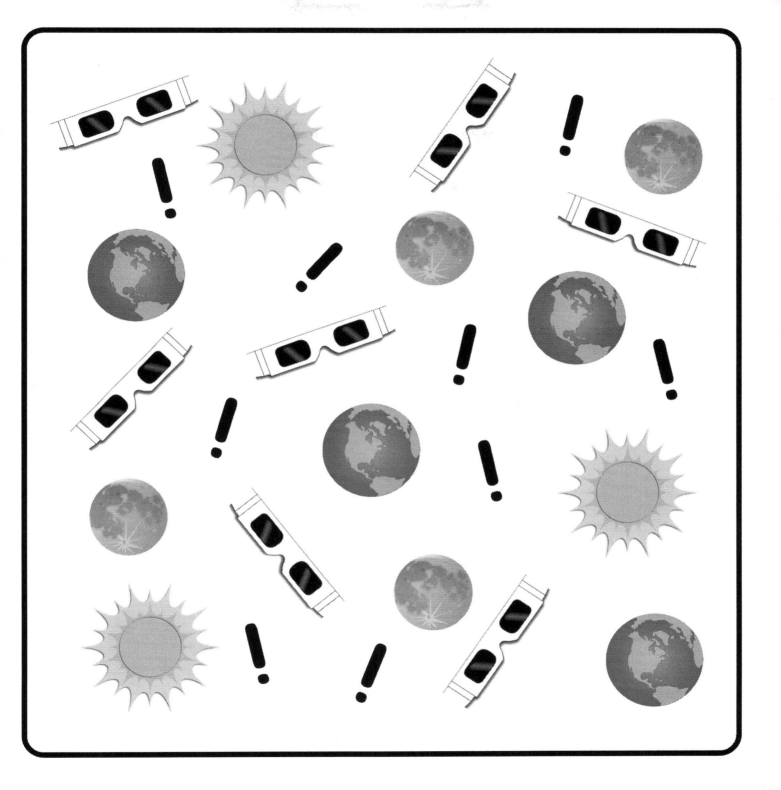

Let's "TRACE the LETTERS"!!!

UPPERCASE

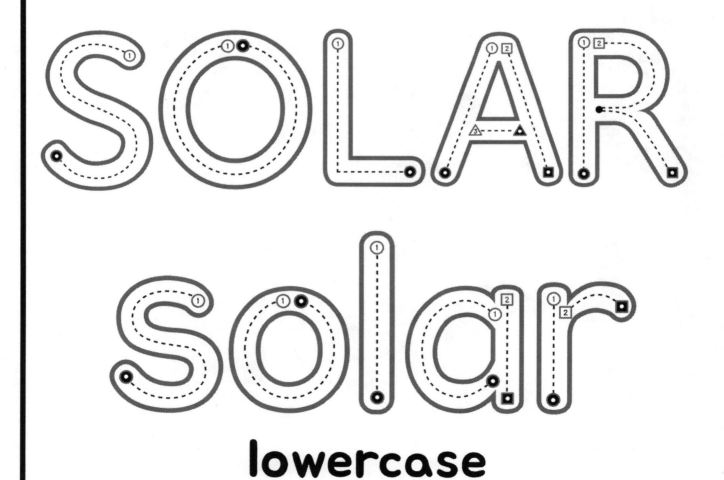

SOLAR

solar

lowercase

If your toddler or preschooler is ready to try "BIG Letter Tracing", then great! Show them how to "follow the guide lines" to write the words SOLAR ECLIPSE. The guide lines are traced in numerical order, starting at the number (as seen below). If your student is not old enough to follow the lines, simply use this page for coloring. Many children are not ready for letter tracing until they are at least 4 or 5 years old, and that is OK :). Always have FUN learning!

START   **STOP**

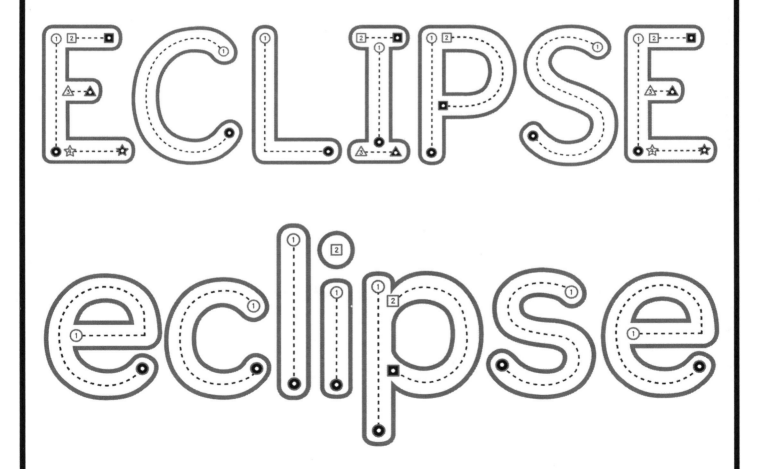

COLOR BY NUMBER!

1 YELLOW
2 ORANGE
3 GREEN
4 BLUE

5 BROWN
6 GRAY
7 BLACK
8 RED
9 PURPLE

EARTH + MOON

GREAT JOB!!!

(A)MAZE(ING)

Mazes are always good for problem solving, pencil control, and fun!

Help the Moon get to the Sun!

HOORAY !!!! You did it !!!!

(A)MAZE(ING)

Help the Eclipse Glasses get to the Earth!

HOORAY !!!! You did it !!!!

STATE SHAPES SEARCH

This is the most advanced activity in this book, and could be difficult for many toddlers and preschoolers. However, it is very fun to do together! Look back at the MAP page and see if you and your student can match the state names with their shapes! Take your time! and draw a line from the state to its name!

TEXAS

OKLAHOMA

KENTUCKY

ARKANSAS

ILLINOIS

MISSOURI

INDIANA

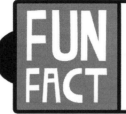

OHIO

MICHIGAN

PENNSYLVANIA

NEW YORK

VERMONT

NEW HAMPSHIRE

MAINE

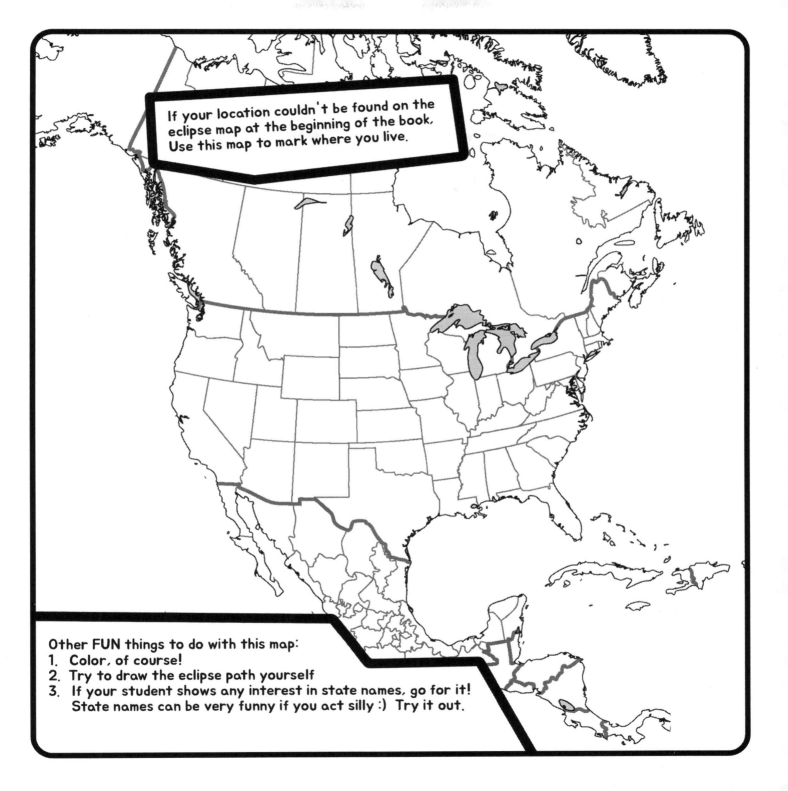

If your location couldn't be found on the eclipse map at the beginning of the book, Use this map to mark where you live.

Other FUN things to do with this map:
1. Color, of course!
2. Try to draw the eclipse path yourself
3. If your student shows any interest in state names, go for it!
   State names can be very funny if you act silly :) Try it out.

My Eclipse Story!

"Tell me your eclipse story, and I will write it down!" Think about: Who was there? What did you see? Where were you? What did you feel? Every story is good!

My Eclipse Picture!

Use this space to draw or color your own picture of the eclipse adventure!

who was there?
what did you see?
where were you?

Made in the USA
Coppell, TX
20 March 2024

30349185R00017